CREATURES THAT GLOW

A Book About Bioluminescent Animals

ISBN 0-590-58108-2

12 11 10 9 8 7 6 5 4 3 2 1   6 7 8 9/9 0 1/0

Printed in the U.S.A.   09

First Scholastic printing, April 1996

Book design by Laurie Williams

CREATURES THAT GLOW

A Book About Bioluminescent Animals

by Melvin Berger

illustrated by Damon Hertig

Scholastic Inc.
New York Toronto London Auckland Sydney

Creatures that glow live almost everywhere.
You can see them —
  — flying through the air,
  — crawling along the ground,
  — swimming in the sea.

Creatures that glow are called
  bioluminescent (bye-oh-loo-meh-NEH-sent).
The word has three parts —
  — *bio* means "life."
  — *lumin* means "light."
  — *escent* means "being."
Bioluminescent creatures are living beings
  that give off light.

But what kind of light do they make?
The glowing creatures' light is not like the
  light of

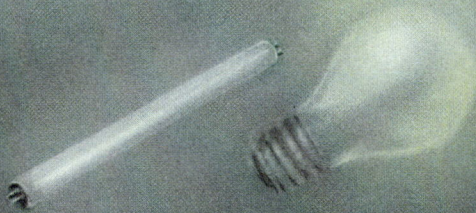

— light bulbs,

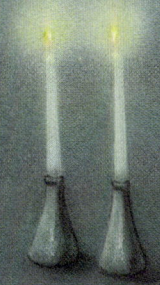

— candles,

— the sun,

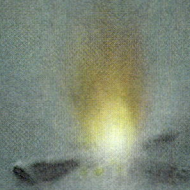

— fire.

This is "hot" light that gives off heat.
Creatures that glow make "cold" light that
  does not give off heat.

Most bioluminescent creatures make their
  own light.
They are born with certain chemicals.
These chemicals mix together in their bodies.
When this happens, the creatures begin
  to glow!

Other creatures that glow cannot make their
    own light.
Instead, they get their light from glowing
    bacteria.

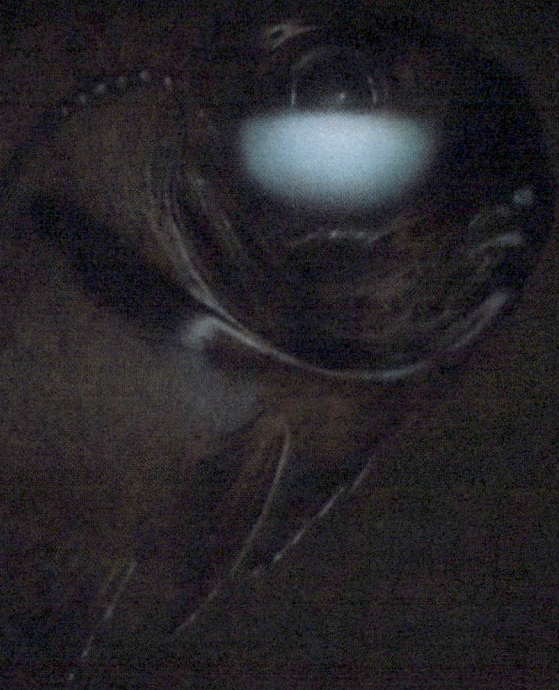

Bacteria are tiny beings.
Certain bacteria make their own light.
Many live inside animals.
Their light shines through the animals' skin.
This makes the animals glow.

Not all bioluminescent creatures are
the same.
Some glow with one color.
Others glow with many colors.

Some lights flash on and off.
Others shine with a steady light.

Some use their light to find mates.
Others use their light to frighten enemies.

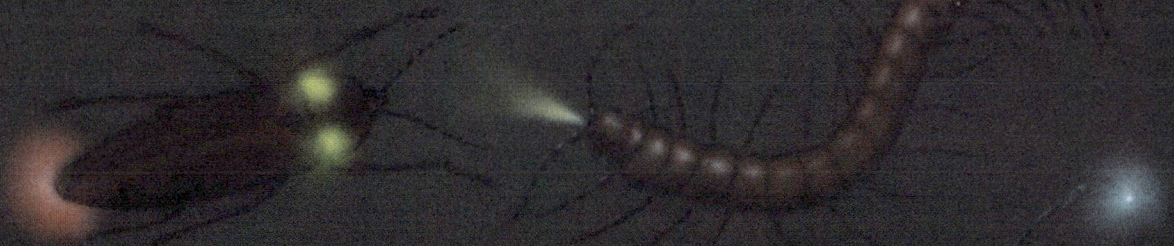

Some glow to light their way.
Others glow to attract prey.

Imagine what life would be like if you
could glow!

Fireflies

Fireflies are also called lightning bugs.
But fireflies are not bugs.
Fireflies are not even flies!
Fireflies are beetles.

Most are about as long as one of your
   fingernails.
During the day they look brown and gray.
But after sunset the back ends light up like
   little lamps!

Fireflies glow with a yellow-white light.
They flash the light on and off.

Fireflies use their light to find mates.
The male flashes his special signal.
The female flashes her answer.

There are many kinds of fireflies.
One kind is called a click beetle.
People sometimes call them fire beetles.
Most click beetles glow with three bright
  lights.
  Two round yellow lights are near the front.
  A red light glows in back.
Can you guess why click beetles are
  sometimes called "auto bugs"?

Click beetles do not flash their lights on
  and off.
Instead, they keep a bright steady light.

Click beetles live in the jungle.
People catch these beetles.
They put them in see-through bags.
And they tie the bags around their ankles
  and wrists.
The glow from the bags helps light their way
  along jungle paths at night.
People also keep click beetles in cages to
  light their homes.

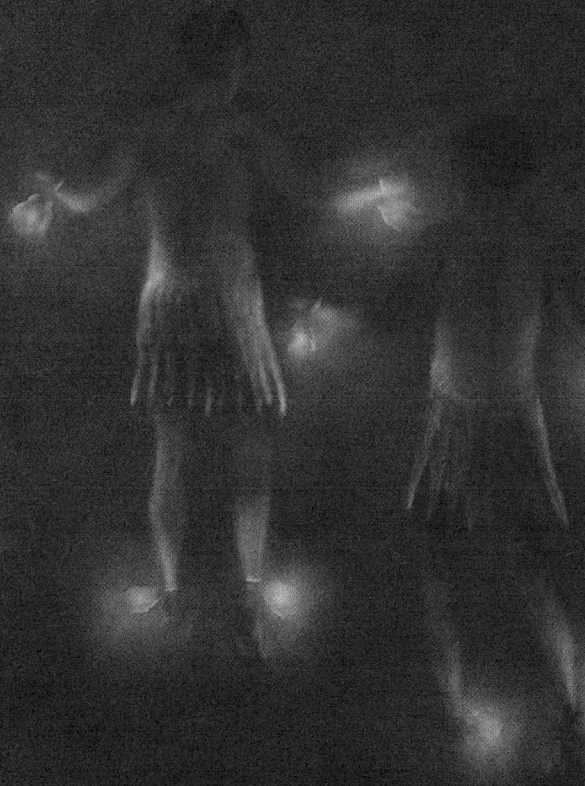

Glowworms

Most glowworms look like short, fat worms.
But they are not worms.
Many glowworms are an early stage in the
life of some insects.

These insects begin life as an egg.
Then the egg hatches, and out crawls a grub.
We call this grub a glowworm.

Glowworms can glow with a bright light.
In time, the grub develops into a fully grown
insect.

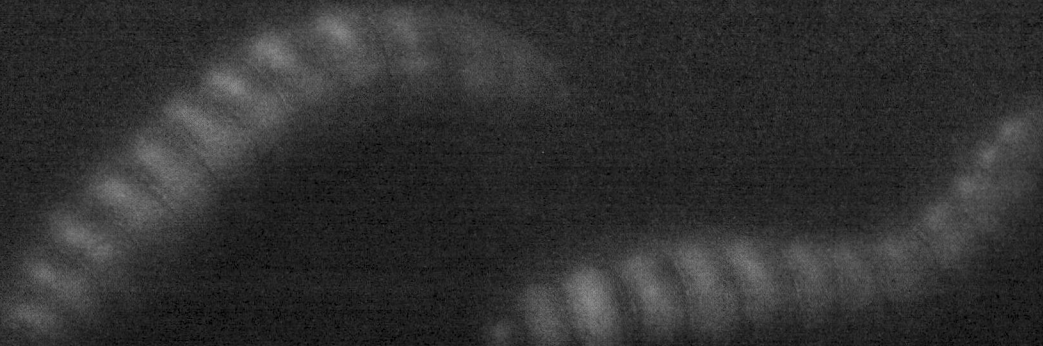

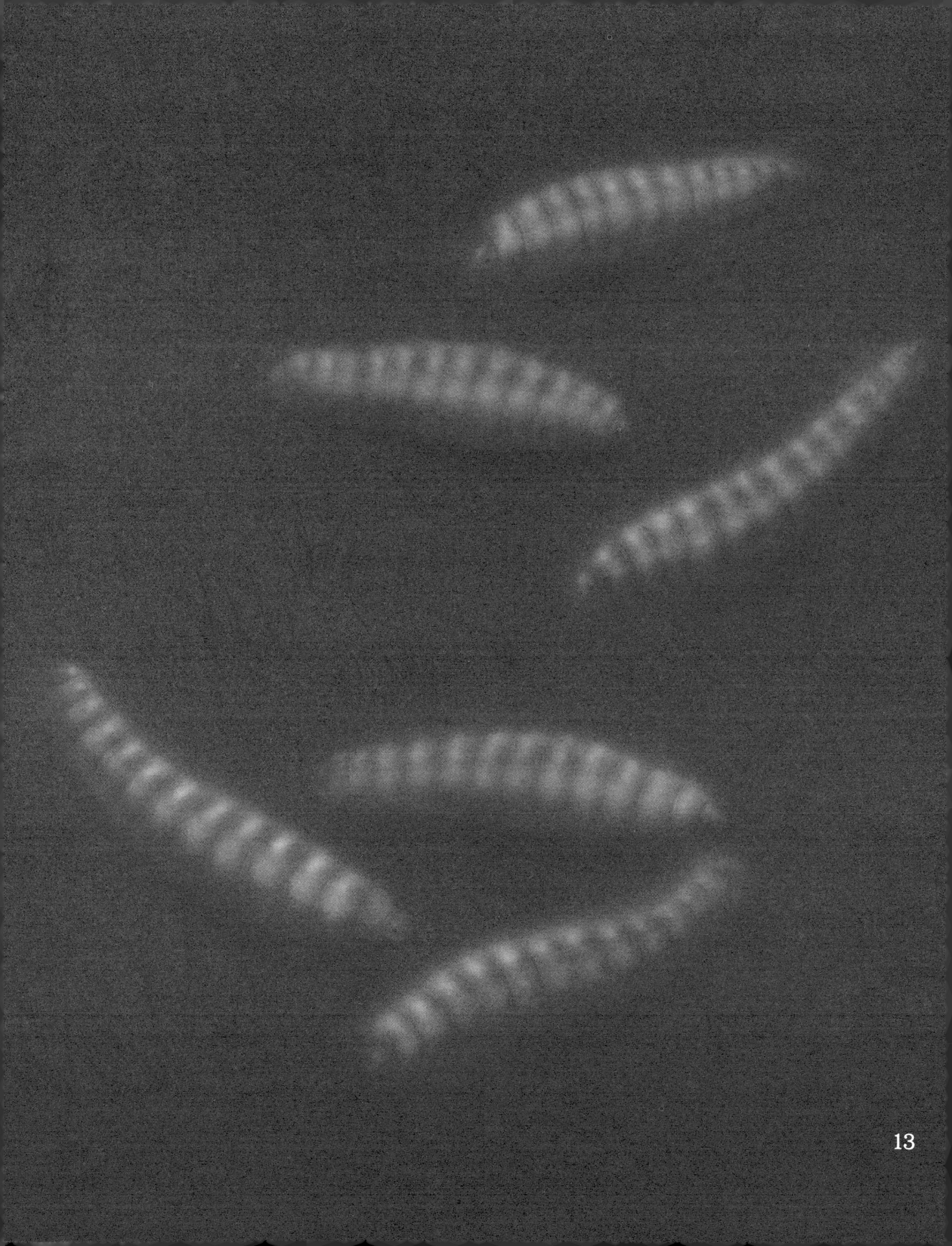

One kind of grub glowworm lives in caves.
It builds small nests that hang from the
cave's roof.
The tiny glowworms group in thousands on
the roof.
The light they make together is bright
enough to read by.

These grub glowworms eat small insects.
They catch the insects in a special way.
They spin their saliva into long, sticky
threads.
The threads dangle from their nests.
The glowworms shine their bright lights.

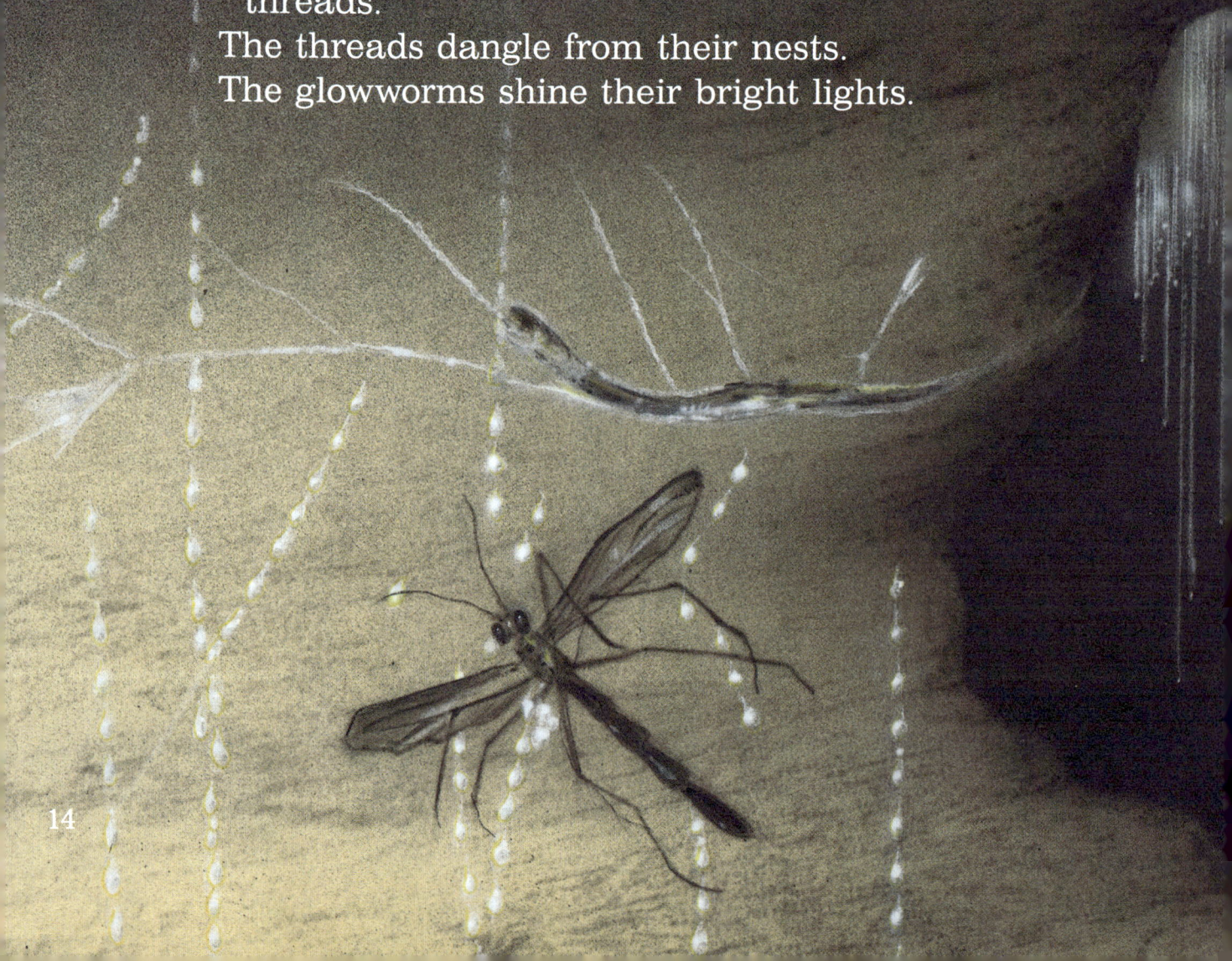

Some insects fly toward the light.
They get caught in the hanging threads.
Quickly the glowworms slide down
 the threads.
Crunch! The glowworms gobble up
 the insects!

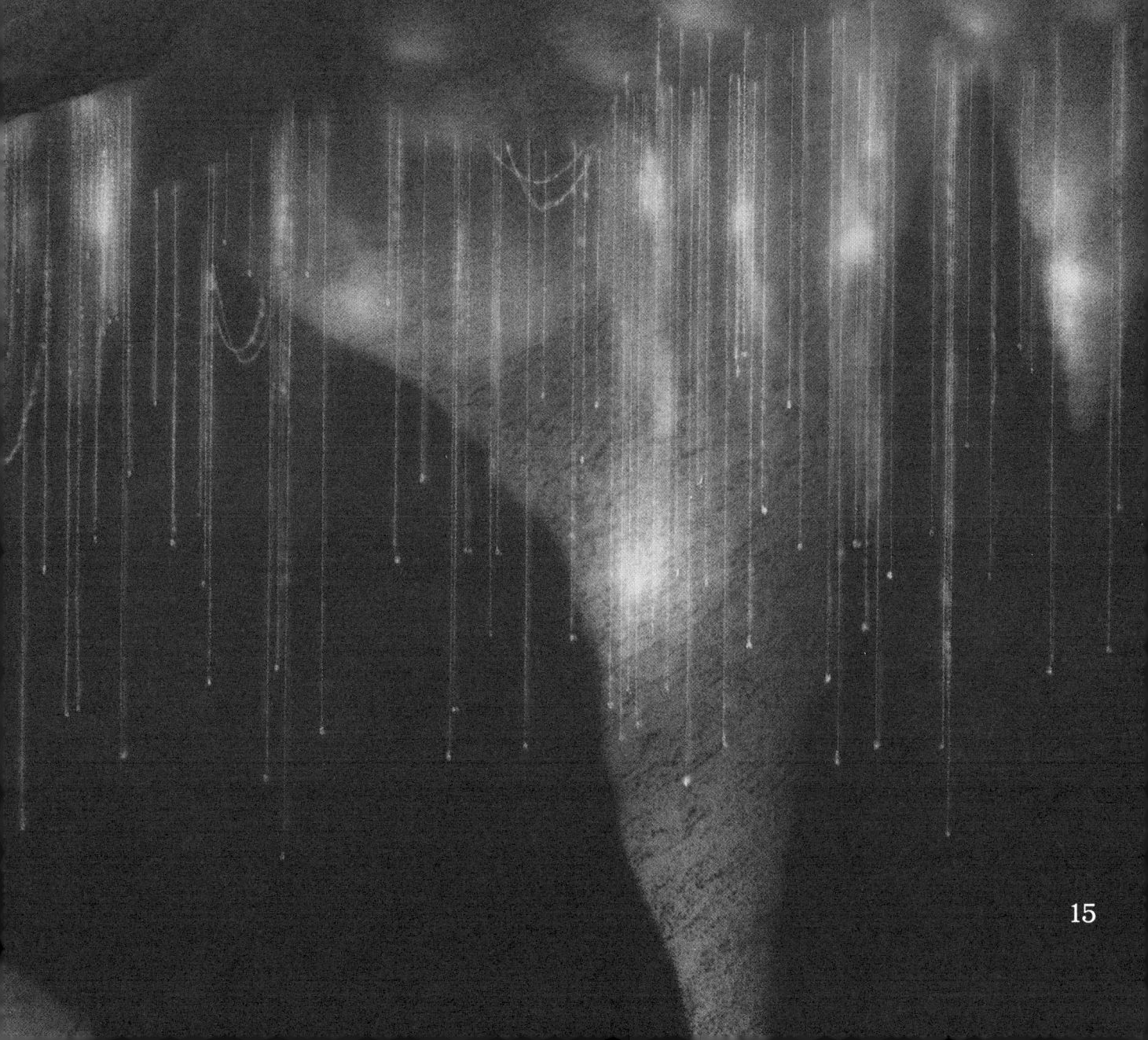

Railroad Worms

Railroad worms are also glowworms.
But they are the *adult* stage of certain
  insects.
Railroad worms are adult beetles without
  wings.

Railroad worms are hard to find.
By day they don't glow.
Often they hide under logs or rocks.

But at night the railroad worms come out.
They start to glow if they are touched.
They also glow if they hear a loud sound.
And they glow with different colors!

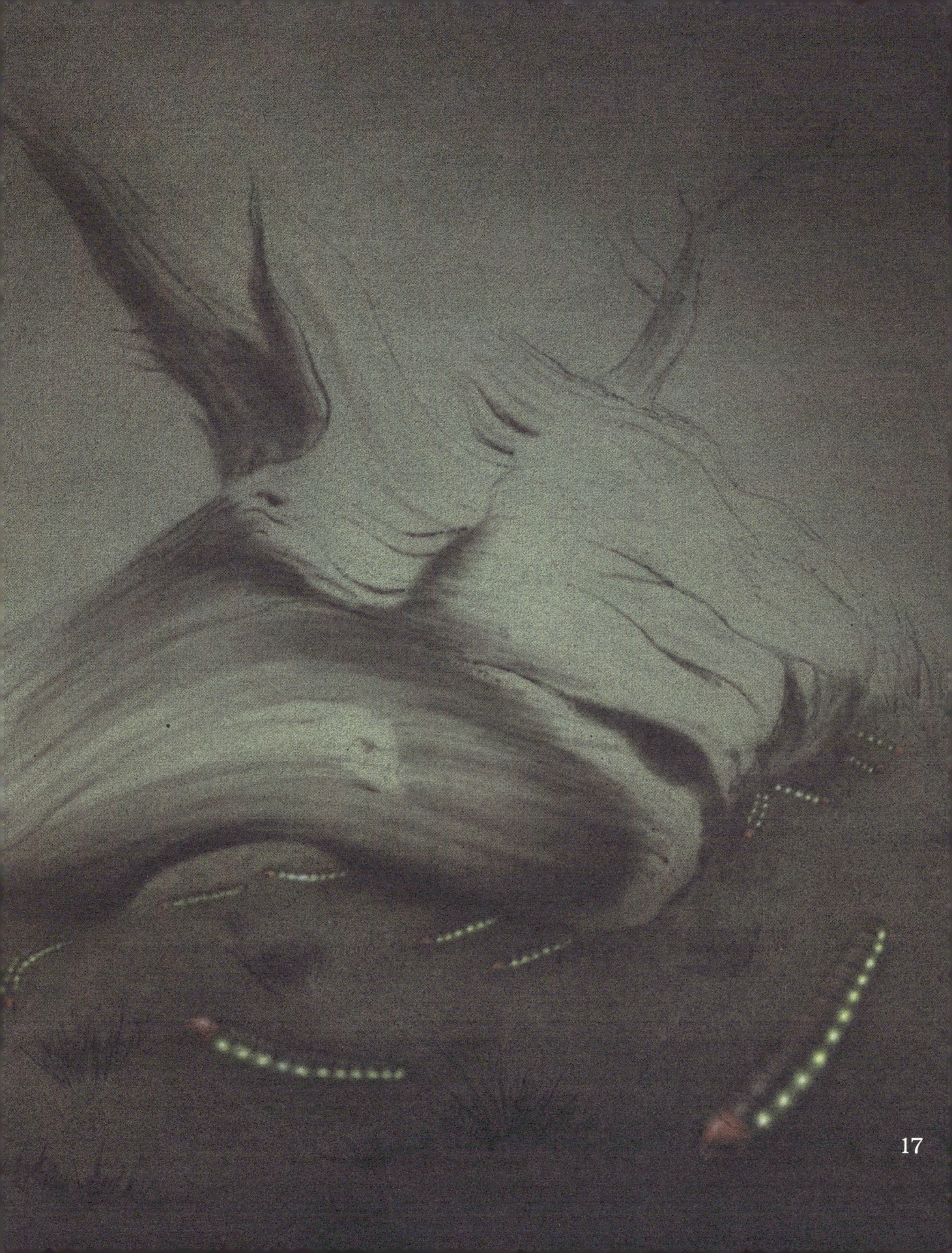

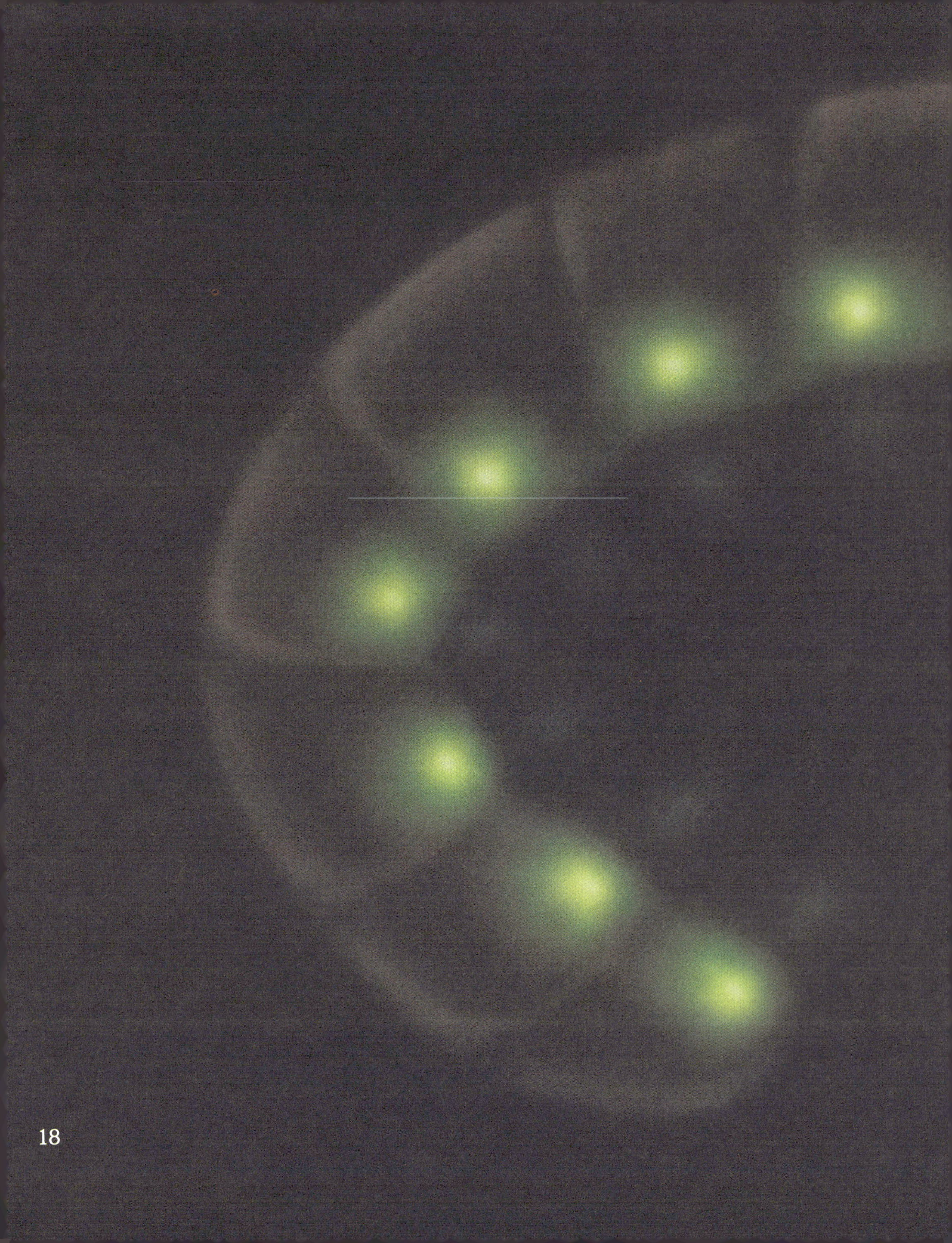

On the head of each railroad worm is a
  bright red light.
It looks something like a train headlight.
Eleven yellow-green lights line each side of
  the body.
The lights look like the windows of a
  night train.

Usually the worms curl up tightly.
At night they look like trains going around
  a curve.

Centipedes

Centipedes look like thin worms with many,
  many legs.
Certain kinds can make their own light.
Their bodies don't glow.
Instead, they give off a poison that glows.

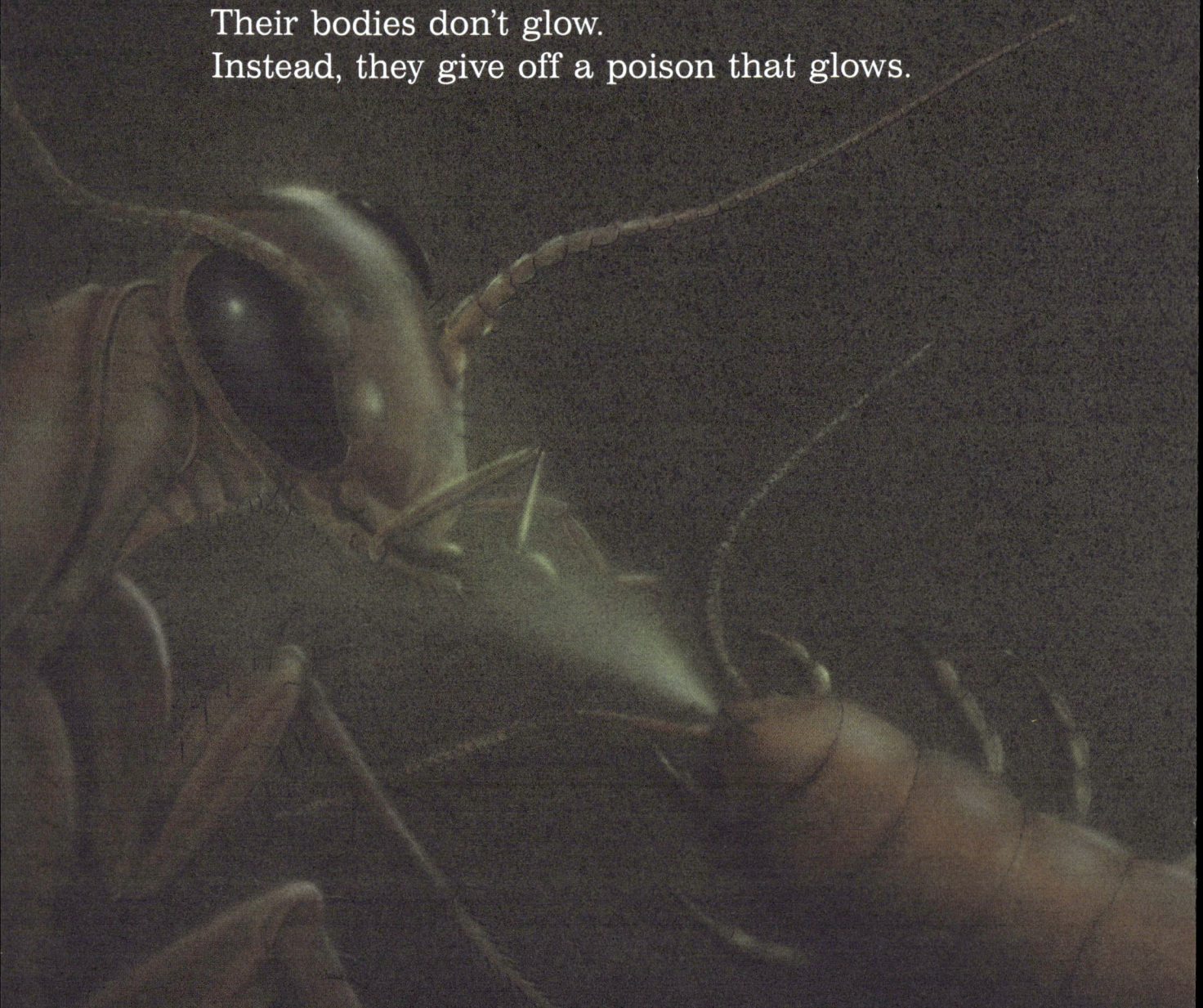

Some bioluminescent centipedes are blind.
Therefore, they cannot see the light
  they make.
So these centipedes can't use their light to
  find mates or food.

Blind centipedes that glow use their light in
  another way.
They use it to scare away enemies.

Suppose an enemy attacks a centipede.
The centipede squirts its glowing poison over
  the enemy.
The poison burns like fire.
And it smells very bad.
The enemy flees.

Later the enemy may spot another
  centipede's glowing poison.
What happens?
The enemy remembers this poisonous glow.
It is a warning to get out of the way — fast!

Jellyfish

Jellyfish are sea animals.
They look like open umbrellas.
The smallest jellyfish are the size of
   your thumb.
The biggest are as wide as a rowboat.

A few kinds of jellyfish give off light.
Jellyfish make their own light.
One type has a few light rings around
   its body.
Another has a border of light spots.
They use their light to find food.
Some small prey see the light of the jellyfish.
They swim toward the light.

Long, thin threads hang from the jellyfish's
   body.
The threads sting the prey that get too close.
Then the jellyfish pulls the prey into
   its mouth.

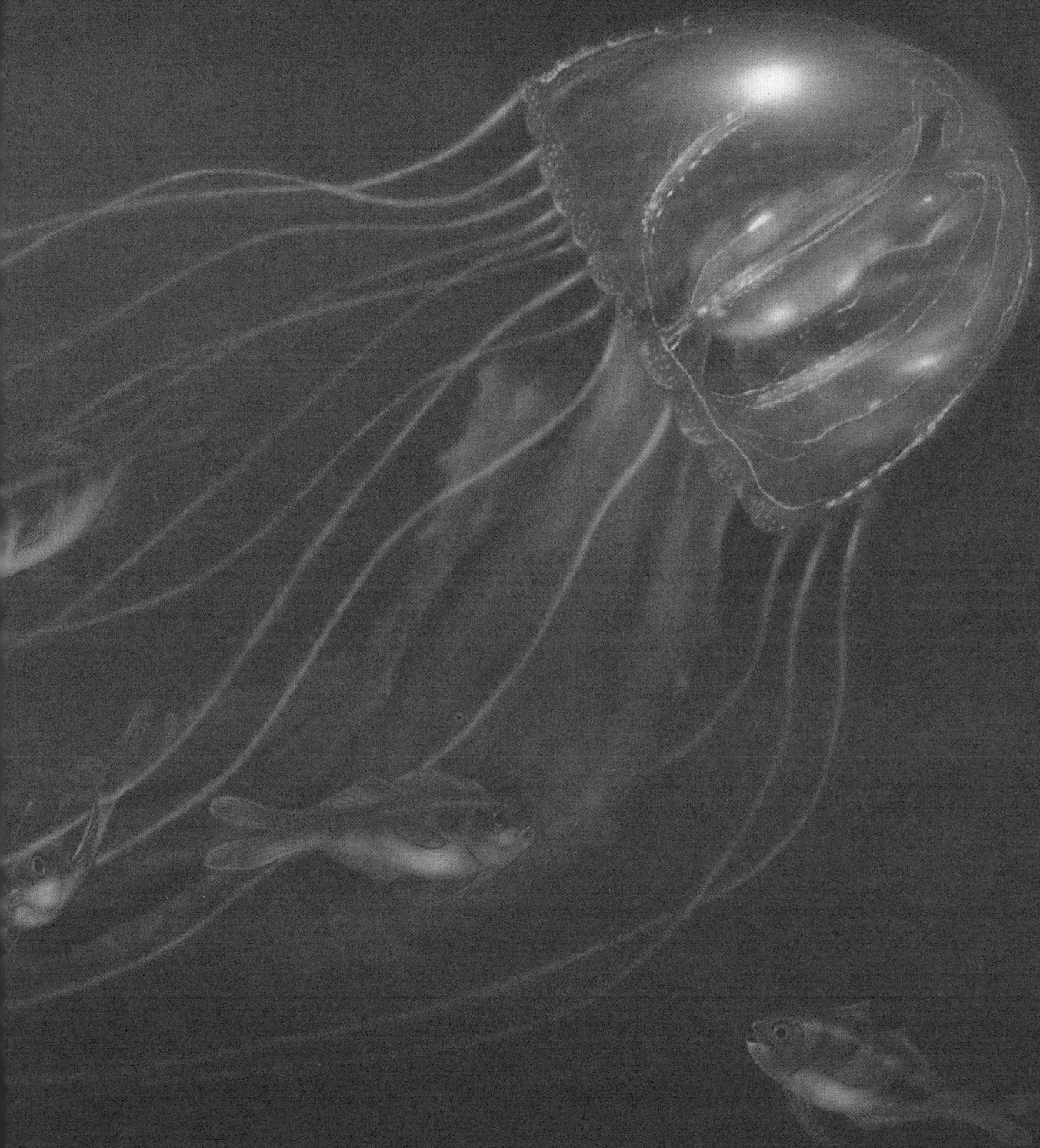

Hatchet Fish

Hatchet fish look just like their name.
They are small and silvery.
And they are shaped like small hatchet
  blades.

These strange creatures live near the
  ocean bottom.
Here it is very, *very* dark.
But the hatchet fish has rows of pink lights
  along the bottom of its body.

Hatchet fish use their light to catch prey.
This is how it works:
A hatchet fish rises to the surface of the
  ocean to chase something to eat.
The rows of pink lights make the fish sparkle
  as it swims along.
It blends in with the water's glistening light,
  made by the sunlight shining from above.

The other fish do not see the hatchet fish.
Some swim too close.
The hatchet fish opens its huge mouth.
Gulp! It swallows the unlucky prey.

Squid

Squid are sea animals that have no bones.
Their bodies are very soft.
Many make their own light.

They use their lights to help them find food.
The lights also help squid find one another.

The deep-sea jeweled squid is very special.
It glows with many colors.
Five lights shine under each of its two
   giant eyes.
      The middle lights are blue.
      The outside lights are gray.

Eight lights shine on the squid's underside.
      The front lights are red.
      The middle lights are blue.
      The back lights are white.

The firefly squid is another squid that glows.
It has many small lights covering its body.
During the day, the creature looks dull
   and spotted.
But at night it glows with many bright
   blue lights.

The bodies of other types of squid do
   not glow.
But they can squirt out a liquid that
   glows blue!
If the squid feels threatened, it squirts the
   glowing liquid into the dark water.
The liquid blinds enemies temporarily.
The squid swims safely away.

Angler Fish

Angler fish live in the deepest part of the
  ocean.
One is small enough to fit in your hand.
But watch out!
Angler fish have great big mouths.
And many sharp teeth line their jaws.
A long rod sticks up from the head of the
  angler fish.
The rod looks like a tiny fishing pole.
At the end of the pole is a blue-green light.
The light dangles in front of the fish.

As an angler fish swims, it flashes its light.
The flashes attract many small sea animals.
These animals come close.
The angler fish opens its mouth.
Snap! In goes dinner.

Flashlight Fish

Flashlight fish are sometimes called "lantern
  eyes."
Both names come from the way these fish
  look.
Under each eye is a small bag of skin.
The bags glow with a bright blue light.
Flashlight fish glow but do not make their
  own light.
Their light comes from billions of tiny,
  glowing bacteria.
The bacteria live *inside* the fish's eye bags.

A bright blue glow shines through the skin of
   the flashlight fish's eye bags.
It makes the bags look like lit lanterns.

The bacteria give off a steady glow.
But what happens when the flashlight fish
   wants to shut off the light?
It covers each bag with a thick fold of skin
   like an eyelid.
This cuts the light off completely.

Flashlight fish use their light in many ways:
   To help them see where they are going.
   To help them search for food.
   To help them find mates.
   Maybe even to help them "talk" to each
      other.

The light also protects the flashlight fish
  from enemies.
Big fish often try to catch flashlight fish.
The flashlight fish try to confuse their
  attackers.
They suddenly shut off the light.
Or the flashlight fish start to zigzag, blinking
  their lights on and off rapidly.
After a while, the enemies give up trying to
  catch the flashlight fish.
They swim away to look for other food.

There are thousands of other bioluminescent
  creatures.
They vary widely in shape and color.
They live in most climates on earth.
And they can be found in all levels of
  the ocean.
So keep an eye out.
You may see some Creatures That Glow.